Astronaut

by Stephen Rickard

Published by Ransom Publishing Ltd.
Radley House, 8 St. Cross Road, Winchester, Hampshire
SO23 9HX, UK
www.ransom.co.uk

ISBN   978 184167 781 1

First published in 2010
Reprinted 2011, 2012

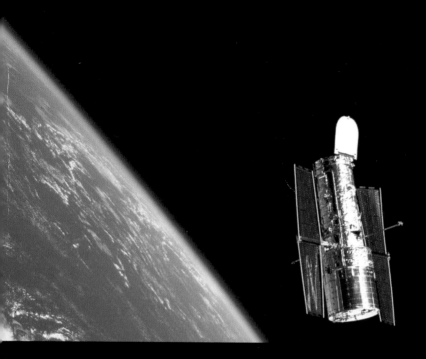

ASTRONAUT

LIFE AT THE
EDGE

STEPHEN RICKARD

Ransom

Main engines.
There are three.

Wings.
Useful for landing.

Cargo bay.
4.6 metres wide
x 18 metres long.

THE SPACE SHUTTLE ORBITER

Cockpit.
Big enough for eleven astronauts
(in an emergency).

SHUTTLE DATA
Length: 37.2 metres
Wingspan: 23.8 metres
Height: 17.9 metres
Speed: 27,870 km/hour (17,320 mph)

Today is flight day. Today we go into space.

We're off to the launch pad now. We go there in this bus. It's called the Astrovan.

NASA

There are seven of us on this trip.

We have spent years training for this. We can pilot the Shuttle. We know what to do if something goes wrong.

The Space Shuttle is ready for us. It is on Launch Pad 39A at NASA's Kennedy Space Centre in Florida, USA.

The Shuttle was built at the Vehicle Assembly Building, three and a half miles away from the launch pad.

Then slowly it was moved to the launch pad. That's called rollout.

Here you can see the rollout.

You can see the launch pad in the distance.

The Shuttle was moved on a very big crawler-transporter.

It took six hours to travel to the launch pad.

This thing is big!

But now it is ready for us. This is for real.

The big orange tank is full of fuel. This fuel is very cold. It is so cold that it makes the tank shrink as it is filled up. I can hear it creaking as we get near the Shuttle.

The Shuttle has three engines. The big orange tank has the fuel for them.

The two big white tubes are called solid rocket boosters. They are extra engines. They give extra power for lift off.

We climb into the Shuttle. People strap us into our seats.

Then they close the hatch and go to a safe place. Like – several miles away.

I am here.

We're on our own. But we have work to do.

Endeavour

T minus 3. It's now three minutes before launch. Power on.

We close the visors on our helmets to protect us from the noise.

T minus 31 seconds. The Shuttle's computers take control.

T minus 6 seconds. The three main engines fire up. Three seconds later they are at maximum thrust.

Everything is shaking like crazy.

T minus zero. Launch. The boosters are lit.

Lift off.

We feel a big kick as the boosters fire. The noise and shaking is almost too much to bear.

T plus 45 seconds. We break the sound barrier. That's 0 – 768 mph in 45 seconds.

Now everything is shaking even harder.

Less than a minute later we are travelling at nearly two thousand miles an hour ...

... at an altitude of 66,000 feet.

T plus 2 minutes. We are now 45 km high. The fuel in the Solid Rocket Boosters is all used up.

Explosive bolts fire and the boosters fall back to Earth. They land in the sea and can be used again.

Now it's just us and the big orange tank full of fuel.

But the engines are still burning several tonnes of fuel every second.

T plus eight minutes. Just eight minutes after launch, and we are in orbit around the Earth.

Now our big orange fuel tank is empty. We don't need it any more.

It falls back to Earth. Most of it will burn up as it enters the atmosphere. The rest lands in the sea.

In orbit, we lose all gravity. I undo my straps and float across the cockpit. We are in space.

We take off our suits and helmets. We can wear normal clothes inside the Shuttle.

We are orbiting about 200 miles above the Earth. We are travelling at 7.68 km per second. That's 17,180 miles per hour.

But it doesn't feel like we are moving at all. The shaking has stopped and everything is quiet.

This is the inside of the shuttle. It's the mid-deck.

It's all a bit messy. It's not like you see in those science fiction movies.

We must tie everything down – or stick it to the walls – or it floats away.

We have four computers to control the Shuttle. They all do the same job.

If one goes wrong, the other three computers ignore it and carry on.

This is our view from the window.

It is awesome.

Utterly fantastic.

It looks nice, but it's not friendly.

If I was outside, I'd live for just 15 seconds.

So my space craft and space suit had better work.

There's no gravity, so for us there's no 'up' or 'down'.

With no gravity, I'm 5 cm taller. That hurts my back.

And most of us get space sick. Being sick in zero gravity is no fun.

That's all I'm saying.

With no gravity, blood rushes to my head. It's like hanging upside down all the time.

My face puffs up and my nose gets blocked.

I can't smell or taste either. But there's no shower on the Shuttle, so it's fine with me that I can't smell anything.

This is the flight deck of the Shuttle. We call it the glass cockpit.

There are 11 computer screens.

Keeping stuff tidy on the Shuttle is really hard. Everything keeps floating out of the drawers.

So we always end up stuffing things in bags and holding them down with bungee cords.

This is where we sleep. It's not called a bed. It's called a sleep station.

We sleep standing up – except that there is no 'up'.

Don't forget – we are here to work.

Sometimes we fix other satellites. This is the International Space Station. The Shuttle comes to visit it now and again.

Sometimes we have to go outside to fix things.

We call that extra-vehicular activity, or EVA for short.

Here is the Shuttle with its cargo doors open.

We usually carry about 22,000 kg of cargo. It's food for the Space Station, or new parts.

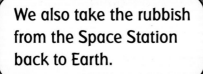

We also take the rubbish from the Space Station back to Earth.

This picture was taken from the International Space Station.

This is how we see the International Space Station as we move away from it.

It looks like a big metal insect.

Then, twelve days later, it's time to go home.

But that's really another story.

JARGON BUSTER

altitude	Kennedy Space
astronaut	Centre
Astrovan	launch pad
atmosphere	NASA
booster	orbit
crawler-transporter	rocket
extra-vehicular	rollout
activity	solid rocket boosters
gravity	Space Shuttle
International Space	thrust
Station	Vehicle Assembly
	Building